The Development of Nottingh
by J.P. Wilson

Midland Counties Railway/Mic

The Midland Counties Railway came into being as the result of the opening of the Leicester & Swannington Railway in July 1832, which resulted in the lowering of the price of coal in Leicester, and as a consequence the loss of this market to the Erewash Valley Coal-owners. At a series of meetings in the autumn of 1832, including one at the Sun Inn, Eastwood, these Coal-owners resolved to construct a line from Pinxton to Leicester (connecting with the Mansfield and Pinxton Tramway, opened in 1819). After two revisions of plans, Lancashire shareholders suggested in 1835 the route should be resurveyed. Chas B. Vignoles was appointed engineer and the plan was now for lines from Derby to Nottingham and from Long Eaton to Rugby (to connect with the London & Birmingham Railway). This was authorised by an Act of June 21, 1836 and by April 1838 the whole line was under contract, and by June the contract for the Nottingham Station had been let.

The Nottingham station-house, engine-house and goods shed were built on meadow land formerly belonging to the Nottingham Corporation, an area of 11 acres of which the station-house occupied about 450 square yards. It was constructed in Grecian style with a facade 90ft. long, the stone obtained from the Heathcote Quarry, Darley Dale. On the top was a stone balustrade surmounted with a scroll and shield bearing the arms of the company. (These were emblems representing the four counties served by the railway ie. Leics, Derbys, Warwicks and Notts). The building faced east and at the rear was a double train-shed 160ft. x 35ft. with an iron roof.

The opening ceremony of the MCR took place on May 30, 1839. The carriages were divided into four trains, six in each of the first three and two in the last, headed by separate engines "Ariel", "Mersey", "Hawk" and "Sunbeam". At half-past twelve "Sunbeam" took its train out of the Nottingham station for Derby, followed five minutes later by "Ariel". Public service commenced on June 4 with four trains each way per day and two on Sundays. Fares were 4/- first class and 2/6 second class for the whole journey, soon to be reduced by 6d in each case.

Further evidence that the railways were establishing themselves in the public's confidence occurred when on July 22, 1840 the Dowager Queen Adelaide (widow of William IV) and her sister Duchess Ida of Saxe-Weinar passed through Nottingham en route from Belton House, Grantham to Harewood House. The Royal cortège of three carriages had come to Nottingham by road and on entering the town over the Trent Bridge had passed along the Flood Road (London Road), Canal Street and over the Navigation Bridge (Wilford Street) to the railway station. A large crowd of spectators was assembled in the station yard and the Dowager Queen remained in the station for about half an hour before passing along the platform to take her seat in the train. This consisted of three Royal carriages belonging to the London and Birmingham Railway and four trucks for

When first opened there was no approach road to the MCR station. Access was gained via a path from Wilford Street near the Navigation Bridge until the Carrington Street Bridge was completed in October 1842. Note the gate-pillars on the right.

conveying the private carriages and luggage van of the Queen and her attendants.

But a greater event was to come for on December 4, 1843 Queen Victoria and the Prince Consort were travelling from Chatsworth House to Belvoir Castle and had entrained at Chesterfield coming over the North Midland Railway to Derby and thence by the Midland Counties Railway to Nottingham. Preparations for a great crowd of sightseers had been made and in the station yard an immense platform in the shape of an inclined plane had been erected. At twenty minutes past eleven the Royal salute boomed from the guns planted on the Castle Rock, announcing that the Royal train was in sight. As it drew into the station the band of the Inniskilling Dragoons struck up the National Anthem and a detachment of the 64th Foot presented arms. The Queen and her Consort alighted and walked along the platform and were formally received by the Lord Lieutenant, the Earl of Scarbrough and the Mayor of Nottingham. In about ten minutes the Queen and the Prince Consort left the station for Belvoir Castle by carriage via the new road across the Westcroft enclosure. The road had been specially completed for the day and from the circumstances of the Royal visit was named Queens Road. Three triumphal arches through which the carriages passed had been erected for the occasion.

These train journeys were among the earliest undertaken by members of the Royal Family.

In 1844 the MCR amalgamated with the North Midland Railway and the Birmingham & Derby Junction Railway to form the Midland Railway. The MR (Nottingham & Lincoln Railway) Act of June 30 1845 authorised the extension of the Derby-Nottingham line. A junction was made near Wilford Road, the new line passing the station on the south side and crossing Queen's Road on

2

the level (Queen's Road at this date extended from the Flood Road to the front of the station).

Section 16 of the MR Act gave power "to carry across and on the level Road No 49 (Queens Road) in the Parish of St. Mary".

Section 17 stated "to cross Nottingham Flood Road by a bridge to leave a clear span between parapet walls of not less than forty feet".

Section 18 required a sufficient bridge for foot passengers across Road No 49.

Section 19 "and whereas the said proposed Branch Railway is intended to cross on the level the said Road No 49, in the Parish of St. Mary, Nottingham aforesaid, at a spot immediately adjoining to a station erected on the said Midland Railway, be it therefore enacted, that all trains on the said Railway shall be made to stop before arriving at such Road and shall not cross the same at any greater speed than Four miles an Hour".

The Nottingham and Lincoln Railway opened ceremonially on August 3, 1846 when two long trains ran from Lincoln to Nottingham where six hundred travellers partook of a magnificent luncheon with a profusion of champagne and other choice wines. The event was presided over by George Hudson "The Railway King".

In November 1846 the Ambergate Railway gave notice of its intention to deviate its projected line through Nottingham and to cross Queens Road on the level. However the Westcroft Committee of the Borough Council entered into negotiations with the Ambergate Railway and reported in March 1847 that the latter were ready to abandon the level-crossing in favour of a line carried on arches across the Meadows.

In November 1848 the Borough Council appointed a Committee to enquire into the right of the MR to have four lines of rails (ie up and down tracks) across Queens Road. The report was published six months later without much satisfaction on the point at issue. (The Act contained no restriction as to the number of lines across the road and it would seem that the Council were under a mistaken impression of the MR Company's intentions) save that the MR were to fix another pair of gates "so constructed as to form a barrier on each side when a train passes". But the crossing continued to be a nuisance and in December 1855 another committee was appointed by the Council to "enquire into the evils of the level-crossing over Queens Road". Again after an interval of six months the report was produced. It stated that trouble arose because the large railway gates were always kept open half way across the carriage road, because two sets of rails were constructed instead of one agreed upon and because of constant shunting on that part of the line crossing the road. An application was made to the Board of Trade who made an order for a year that the gates be kept closed across the railway except when trains were passing. Consideration was also given to proceeding by indictment to compel the MR to remove the extra line of rails and to discontinue shunting.

By April 1861 an agreement was reached between the Borough Council and the MR to replace the Wilford Road crossing by a bridge thirty six-feet wide. In the following year the MR were making preparations for a proposed viaduct over the Queens Road level-crossing but powers were not obtained until 1866 and the work was not commenced until 1868. It was finally completed about September 1869, the cost was borne by the MR although the Borough Council contributed by way of a bonus of land.

With the Lincoln line in operation the old MCR station became increasingly inadequate, the trains to and from Lincoln having to back into and out of the station although a temporary improvement was provided by new platforms with an all-over gabled roof outside the south wall of the station and immediately on the west side of the crossing.

However, an entirely new station was soon put in hand, situated towards the east end of Station Street, the entrance faced north and covered an area of 600ft. x 94ft. The station opened on May 22, 1848 and remained in use until the present station facing west on to Carrington Street, opened on January 17, 1904.

A further extension was opened up, the Leen Valley from Mansfield Junction, Lenton, to Kirkby on October 2, 1848 and on to Mansfield October 9, 1849.

Queen's Road crossing, looking North c.1860, photo by Samuel Bourne. The railway crosses the road where the group of 4 people are standing (centre). A white signal post can be seen above the street lamp and a crossing gate in front of the gabled building on left.

The approach to Nottingham Midland Station from a Wilford Road viewpoint. The site of the MCR station was approximately in the second bay from the right of the goods warehouse. The curve of the Lincoln line extension of 1846 to the south side of the station can be clearly seen.

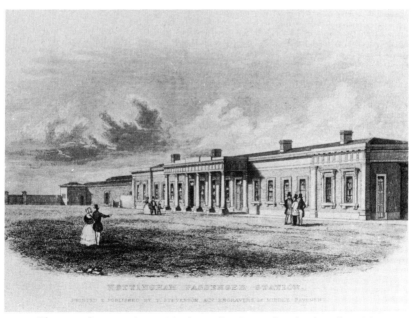

The second MR station, 1848 in Station Street, it existed until 1904.

The Midland Station frontage c. 1930. Compare with similar view of Queen's Road crossing.

The completion of the viaduct coincided with other alterations and improvements at the station, including a third platform and new goods lines on the south side following the acquisition and filling-in of the Westcroft branch canal (constructed under an Act of July 4, 1839). The viaduct altered the relative levels of the road and adjacent buildings. The Victoria Hotel (later renamed the Bentinck Hotel) at the corner of Station Street., was elevated by another floor with a new entrance on the former first floor. A similar reconstruction took place at the Queen's Hotel at the corner of Queen's Walk and Arkwright Street. Evidence of this can be seen to this day.

The old station, described as being ''in a half-drowned position'' since the building of the viaduct, was demolished in 1875 and replaced by a new building which served as the goods offices for many years and still stands. The gate pillars leading to the yard would appear to be part of the original station, although the capping stones have been damaged and replaced by bricks. At the time of demolition the stone coat of arms was removed to the garden of 83 Queen's Drive, then the residence of Mr. Johnson the stationmaster. It remained until the house itself was demolished and was rescued in the nick of time and taken to the Industrial Museum at Wollaton Hall.

Further lines were opened in connection with the MR's desire to develop its Anglo-Scottish traffic starting with the Radford-Trowell on May 1, 1875. In the same year a new large locomotive shed at Middle Furlong Road was completed. Acts of 1872-74 authorised the construction of the 18 mile line from London Road junction to Melton Junction, which with other links

Arms of the MCR. Only the NOTTINGHAM Town arms, top right was a coat of arms, the rest were emblems associated with LEICESTERSHIRE, top left, DERBYSHIRE lower left, WARWICKSHIRE, lower right. (Photo: G.H.F. Atkins)

Gate pillars of the MCR station still in situ.

effectively created a new main line to St. Pancras, 123½ miles in length. Goods traffic commenced on November 1, 1879, passenger traffic on February 2, 1880. Through expresses from St. Pancras to Bradford followed on June 1, 1880 and finally Anglo-Scottish services were inaugurated in February 1882.

As a result of the building of the Great Central Railway's London Extension and the opening of its impressive Renaissance styled Victoria Station in May 1901 the MR was compelled to rebuild its own early Victorian station. The MR selected the architect of Victoria Station, A.E. Lambert. The 1848 station was virtually swept away, platform sites were extended westwards towards the new one-storey frontage in red sandstone and terra-cotta on Carrington Street Bridge which had been rebuilt and widened. The opening took place on January 17, 1904 and the structure remains basically the same to this day, its impressive wrought-iron gates in the Art Nouveau style set out an arcaded porte-cochére. Lambert produced an emphatically Edwardian facade similar to his later designs for the Albert Hall Methodist Mission (1907-9).

As a result of the Beeching proposals for rationalisation the express trains via the Melton line ceased on April 18, 1966. The line was closed on November 4, 1968 and severed at Edwalton. The effect has been to make Nottingham station a terminus for the London trains routed via Leicester. The few through trains to and from Sheffield having to reverse in the station.

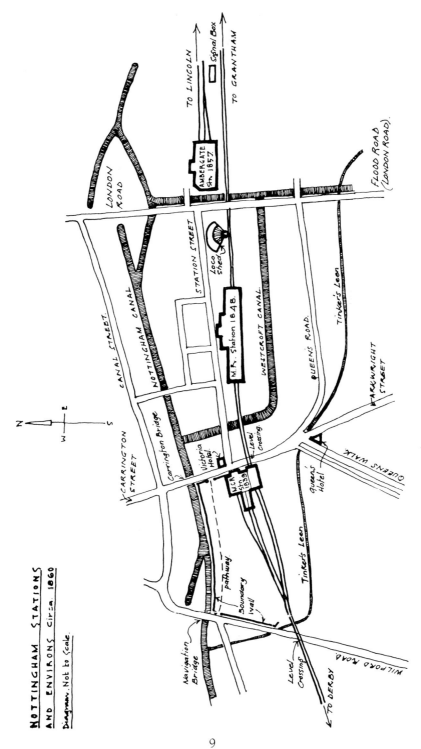

NOTTINGHAM STATIONS
AND ENVIRONS Circa 1860

Diagram. Not to scale.

TO LINCOLN

Signal Box

TO GRANTHAM

AMBERGATE Stn. 1857

LONDON ROAD

FLOOD ROAD (LONDON ROAD)

STATION STREET

Loco Shed

CANAL STREET

NOTTINGHAM CANAL

M.R. Station 1848.

WESTCROFT CANAL.

QUEENS ROAD.

Tinker's Leen

ARKWRIGHT STREET

CARRINGTON STREET

Carrington Bridge

Victoria Hotel

Level Crossing.

Queen's Hotel

QUEENS WALK

M.C.R. Stn 1839

pathway

Boundary Wall

Tinker's Leen

Navigation Bridge

Level Crossing

WILFORD ROAD

TO DERBY

N E S W

A Derby train awaiting departure from No. 4 platform, Midland. The GC main line bridge, upper foreground, a bowstring girder of 170 feet span went clear across the MR lines.

Ambergate, Nottingham & Boston & Eastern Junction Railway/Great Northern Railway

The history of this line goes back to 1845 when plans were being put forward for a trunk line between Manchester and the East Coast ports of Boston and King's Lynn. The North-Western and separate company was the Manchester, Buxton, Matlock & Midlands Junction Railway, the two concerns joining at Ambergate with the MR. The Ambergate Railway obtained its Act on July 6, 1846 which authorised a line from Ambergate through Nottingham and Spalding to Boston with branches therefrom. These schemes were among scores conceived in the "Railway Mania" years of 1845-6, and inevitably the market collapsed and many were abortive. The MBM and MJR was left with 11 miles between Ambergate and Rowsley, whilst the Ambergate was confined to 19 miles from a terminus at Earle's Field, Grantham to a junction with the MR at Colwick, running powers having been obtained over the MR line to their Nottingham station.

In 1849 an Act was obtained to relinquish its powers for construction west of Nottingham and the line to Boston and Sleaford. The opening ceremony of the Grantham-Colwick line took place on July 15, 1850 at Earle's Field station.

The Ambergate Railway had become a link between the MR and GNR and there soon developed a struggle between the two companies for control of the Ambergate. Following the opening of the GNR "Towns Line" from Werrington Junction, Peterborough to Retford on August 1, 1852 a through service was advertised between King's Cross and Nottingham in less time than the MR. The first train was drawn into the Nottingham station by a GNR engine. It was then "surrounded" by MR engines, taken into their shed and access rails removed. Seven months elapsed before the locomotive was returned. The MR continued to be obstructive and refused to accept through traffic, which meant that the Ambergate Railway had to convey goods to Colwick by cart. None of their engines were allowed to pass over the MR lines without a certificate from the latter's engineer.

Acts of 1853 and 1854 empowered the Ambergate Railway to 1. Abandon the projected lines east of Grantham. 2. To amalgamate with the GNR. 3. To construct an independent line from Colwick to Nottingham with a station at the Eastcroft. From April 4, 1853 the GNR took over all rolling stock and other effects on a 999 year lease.

The new station at London Road, and the 3 mile line, together with a goods and corn warehouse were opened on October 3, 1857. Designed by T.C. Hine and erected by J. Ferguson, the station comprised a range of offices on the north and west sides and a wall on the south, the whole enclosing the train shed and covering the arrival and departure platforms. The goods and corn warehouse some 200 yards to the east was a two storey building, the lower 200ft. by 80ft. for goods and the upper for corn. Two thirds of the upper floor was suspended by iron rods from the roof in order to keep the lower floor as free as possible from any obstruction.

The haulage of coal by rail to the London coal market was beginning to become an important and lucrative traffic. Thus the development of the Notts

The ornate Ambergate Railway's terminus at London Road, dating from 1857. Recently faithfully restored.

and Derbys coalfield at this time principally along both sides of the Erewash Valley started another source of conflict between the MR and GNR. From 1857 the MR route to London was via Leicester, Bedford and Hitchin and thence over the GNR main line. Naturally the GNR allowed precedence to their own traffic and this spurred the MR to construct its own route to London south of Bedford. This was opened to St. Pancras in 1867.

Already in 1863 the GNR had deposited a Bill for an extension from Nottingham to Codnor Park but this was withdrawn by agreement on coal rates with the MR. But following the completion of the MR trunk line they withdrew the agreement on the GNR through rates on March 24, 1871. In consequence the GNR sought and obtained their Derbyshire & Staffordshire Act on July 25, 1872. This enabled the GNR to reach Awsworth and Pinxton in 1875 and thence from a junction at Awsworth to Derby and Egginton Junction in 1878. From here by acquiring running powers over the North Staffordshire Railway the GNR reached Burton-on-Trent in 1881 and subsequently Stafford.

In order to attain these westerly destinations it had been necessary to branch off from Netherfield Junction three and a half miles east of the London Road terminus and describe a semi-circle involving a steep ascent to Mapperley tunnel.

The GNR was seeking to develop in other directions, first through the Vale of Belvoir and beyond to tap the iron-ore deposits. By means of agreement with the London & North Western Railway they established a Joint Line from Newark to Melton Mowbray and Market Harborough with a spur from Saxondale Junction to Harby and Stathern. These lines were opened 1878-1880 eventually giving a Nottingham-Northampton passenger service worked by the LNWR. The second project was a line up the Leen Valley to Newstead, inaugurated in 1881-2, in order to serve collieries now opening there, as the older pits in the Erewash Valley became worked out.

In 1886 a group of Nottingham businessmen formed the Nottingham Surburban Railway Company to build a 3¼ mile line from a junction with the GNR at Trent Lane to a junction with the latter's Derbyshire line east of Daybrook Station. Engineering works were heavy and costly, four tunnels, Sneinton, Thorneywood, Sherwood and Ashwells were needed and even so the line rose almost continuously from Trent Lane on gradients of 1 in 49 and 1 in 50 to the southern end of Sherwood tunnel. Although providing a shorter route than the line via Gedling, the gradients proved an obstacle to most of the heavy traffic. Local traffic never developed as anticipated. Electric trams soon became a competitor and passenger traffic ceased in 1916 as a wartime measure.

The engineer was Edward Parry of Woodthorpe Grange, later to be in charge of the Northern section of the Great Central's London extension. The excellence of construction and the lavish use of blue bricks gave him valuable experience for the later project.

Amber Gate, Nottingham and Boston, and Eastern Junction Railway.

NOTTINGHAM AND GRANTHAM.

TIME-TABLE FOR JULY, 1850.

GREENWICH TIME IS KEPT AT ALL THE STATIONS.

STATIONS.	Miles	DOWN. Nottingham to Grantham. 1	2	3	4	Sundays. 1	2	FARES from Nottingham			
		1st 2nd and 3rd Class	1st 2nd & Gov.	Express	1st 2nd and 3rd Class	1st 2nd & Gov.	1st 2nd and 3rd Class	1st Class s. d.	2nd Class s. d.	3rd Class s. d.	4th Class s. d.
Departure from		a. m.	p. m.	p. m.	p. m.	a. m.	p. m.				
Nottingham	...	10 10	1 15	3 45	9 5	9 0	8 0	...	...	...	...
Ratcliffe	5½	10 25	1 39	3 58	9 20	9 16	8 16	1 6	1 0	0 6	0 5½
Bingham	9	10 37	1 56	4 8	9 33	9 30	8 30	2 3	1 6	0 9	0 9
Aslockton	10½	10 42	2 4	4 13	9 39	9 36	8 36	2 7	1 9	0 11	0 10½
Elton	13	10 49	2 14	4 20	9 47	9 44	8 44	3 3	2 2	1 1	1 1
Bottesford	15½	10 58	2 28	4 29	9 56	9 54	8 54	3 11	2 7	1 4	1 3½
Sedgebrook	18½	11 6	2 43	4 36	10 5	10 4	9 4	4 7	3 1	1 7	1 6½
Grantham	22½	11 15	3 0	4 45	10 15	10 15	9 15	5 0	3 9	1 11	1 10½

STATIONS.	Miles	UP. Grantham to Nottingham. 1	2	3	4	Sundays. 1	2	FARES from Grantham.			
		1st 2nd and 3rd Class	1st 2nd & Gov.	Express	1st 2nd and 3rd Class	1st 2nd & Gov.	1st 2nd and 3rd Class	1st Class s. d.	2nd Class s. d.	3rd Class s. d.	4th Class s. d.
Departure from		a. m.	a. m.	p. m.	p. m.	a. m.	p. m.				
Grantham	...	8 40	11 0	2 20	7 0	7 30	6 30	...	...	...	...
Sedgebrook	4½	8 53	11 18	2 30	7 12	7 43	6 43	1 3	1 0	0 6	0 4½
Bottesford	7	9 3	11 34	2 38	7 22	7 53	6 53	1 9	1 2	0 7	0 7
Elton	9½	9 12	11 46	2 45	7 30	8 2	7 2	2 5	1 7	0 10	0 9½
Aslockton	12½	9 20	11 56	2 51	7 38	8 10	7 10	3 0	2 0	1 1	1 0½
Bingham	13½	9 28	12 6	2 57	7 46	8 18	7 18	3 5	2 3	1 2	1 1½
Ratcliffe	17½	9 42	12 24	3 8	7 58	8 32	7 32	4 8	2 11	1 6	1 6½
Nottingham	22½	9 55	12 46	3 20	8 10	8 46	7 45	5 0	3 9	1 11	1 10½

PASSENGERS LUGGAGE.—The Company do not hold themselves responsible for Luggage, unless Booked and paid for according to its value.—100 lbs. weight of Luggage is allowed to First Class, 60 lbs. weight to Second Class, and 40 lbs. weight to Third Class Passengers, not being Merchandise, or any other Articles carried for hire or profit; any excess above that weight will be charged.

The Company do not GUARANTEE the arrival of the Trains at the respective Stations at the times stated, but will use their best endeavours TO ENSURE PUNCTUALITY.

JOHN GOUGH, Secretary.

Manchester, Sheffield & Lincolnshire Railway/Great Central Railway

The MSLR was originally a cross-country line from Manchester to Grimsby with a number of branches, including one south of Sheffield to Beighton. The London coal market was an attraction from the 1860's but three Bills for a "coal-line" failed by 1872. Edward Watkin, Chairman of the MSLR then turned his attention to the idea of a Channel Tunnel, having promoted his own company with the larger plan of a through service between Liverpool and Paris. Boring began in 1880 but opposition on military grounds led to a veto by the Board of Trade and from 1882 the project was abandoned.

Watkin was still determined to get to London. An Act of 1889 authorised a line from Beighton to Annesley, opened in 1893. Further expansion southwards by a Bill of 1890 met with opposition but negotiations with the GNR followed. They were offered running powers over the MSLR west of Sheffield and north of Nottingham plus a half-share in the new "Central Station" in Nottingham if they agreed not to oppose a new Bill. They could hardly refuse and on March 25, 1893 the Act authorised the construction of a 92 mile line from Annesley to Quainton Road (6 miles north-west of Aylesbury) there to effect an end-on junction with the Metropolitan Railway, plus the GNR Leen Valley Extension to Langwith, (Shirebrook). Edward Parry was the engineer for the Annesley to Rugby section, Logan & Hemmingway the contractors for the difficult 19½ miles from Annesley to East Leake.

Bulwell Viaduct, looking North. It was 420 yards long, with 26 arches, needed 6½ million bricks and was completed in 12 months. The spur to the GN Leen Valley Line is in the foreground.

The London-bound "South Yorkshireman" entering Victoria Station, June 1949. It started at Bradford Exchange Station and came via Huddersfield, Penistone and Sheffield.

Bulwell Viaduct of 26 arches and 420 yards long needed 6½ million bricks and was completed in 12 months. Open land followed to Sherwood Rise tunnel, 665 yards, Carrington Station then the Mansfield Road tunnel, 1189 yards which opened onto the station site 650 x 100 yards stretching from Woodborough Road to Parliament Street and from Mansfield Road to Huntingdon Street (then Windsor Street). The clearance of this site involved the demolition of 1300 houses, 20 public houses, the Union Workhouse built in 1840, the Ragged School, and St. Stephen's Church, Sunday School and Hall.

The cost of the land was £473,000 whilst 609,000 cubic yards of earth were taken out to form the station area. To the south of the station area Victoria Street tunnel 393 yards, was constructed by the "cut and cover" method. Thurland Street was excavated to the required depth, the buildings on either side shored up, the concentric rings of brickwork forming the tunnel built up and then covered over and the street surface restored. The line emerged from the tunnel and in the face of the cliff at Weekday Cross and out onto a viaduct across the Marsh, crossing the Midland Station at right angles by a bowstring girder bridge of 170ft. span. Another viaduct took the line through the Meadows, associated work included Arkwright Street Station, a goods depot, an engine shed and sidings. The River Trent was crossed by a bridge of three lattice girders, each of 112ft. span for both main and relief lines. Approach viaducts were constructed at each end.

The GC bridge over the River Trent at Wilford. The goods line turned off at the signal-box making 4 lines over the bridge. All was recently demolished.

An early view of Victoria station and hotel. The elaborate ironwork on the new Centre tramway standards can be seen.

The course taken by the railway south of Victoria Station and through Victoria Street tunnel to emerge at Weekday Cross resulted in the demolition of the old Town Hall. The High Pavement school behind the High Pavement Chapel moved to new premises in Forest Fields. Several old cells and some skeletons were revealed in cutting through the Town Hall (Old Guildhall) site.

The GCR main line was opened to goods traffic on July 25, 1898 and to passenger traffic on March 15, 1899. Northbound trains went through the Joint Station, still uncompleted, to Carrington Station and southbound trains to Arkwright Street Station. The completed station was opened on May 24, 1900 and was named Victoria on the suggestion of the Town Clerk as it coincided with the Queen's birthday.

Victoria Station frontage was on Mansfield Road and extended for 250ft. As noted it was designed in the renaissance style and constructed partly of Darley Dale stone and partly of Nottingham brick. The most prominent feature was the clock tower, (now the sole remaining part of the station). Within, the two island platforms each had north and south bays, the whole 1270ft. long. The glass roof was 420ft. long in three spans, rising to 42ft. 6 ins. above the platform level. Dining and refreshment rooms were provided on both main platforms. Lines for through traffic were between the up and down outer platforms and the station walls.

The work was directed by Edward Parry, with his assistants F.W. Bidder, A.E. Lambert and A.A. Barker. The building of the station was carried out by Henry Lovatt of Wolverhampton.

The opening of Victoria Station meant the transfer of all GNR passenger trains from London Road Station. The Grantham trains were re-routed via a

London Road (High Level) station and Viaduct looking east towards Sneinton. (Photo: J.F. Henton)

new spur from Weekday Cross Junction to Trent Lane Junction and called at the new station of London Road (High Level). The majority of the Derby trains now went via the GC main line to Bagthorpe Junction using the new spurs there, thus shortening the circuitous journey via Gedling. Some of the Pinxton trains were similarly routed.

The old station was henceforth known as London Road (Low Level), which the LNW trains to and from Northampton continued to use until May 12, 1944 when they, too, transferred to Victoria.

The last train from Victoria Station was a Diesel Multiple Unit to Rugby on Saturday, September 2, 1967, after which the service was cut back to Arkwright Street Station and was finally withdrawn on May 5, 1969. Thus ended the dream of Edward Watkin. When the GC was born it had been said MS & L meant "Money sunk and lost" and GC meant "Gone completely". Time proved this to be all too true in spite of a dynamic and competitive spirit. It was the story of a loser.

Sadly too, its priceless asset of a route through the heart of Nottingham has virtually been destroyed. The original plan for retention as a freight-only route with a pair of tracks on the east side of Victoria Station had hardly been carried out when it was hastily abandoned.

The Victoria Station site was developed as a shopping precinct, the viaduct through the Meadows has been demolished, along with the bridge over the River Trent. Northwards in the Valley Road area the extensive railway network has been obliterated and Bulwell Viaduct has been pulled down. Thus any hope of an alternative transport system has been finally extinguished.

Nottingham: Suburbs and Suburban

K.2. 61737 on Nottingham-Skegness Excursion passing under Suburban line flyover at Trent Lane Junction, Nottingham. *(18/7/54)*

Trent Lane Junction looking east. *(7/8/54)*

Lenton Station on the Midland line.   *c.1850*

The 2.08 p.m. ex Basford entering Thorneywood Station hauled by G.N. 0-4-4T 822 (WDN before 1923). (Photo: F.H. Gillford, 1911).

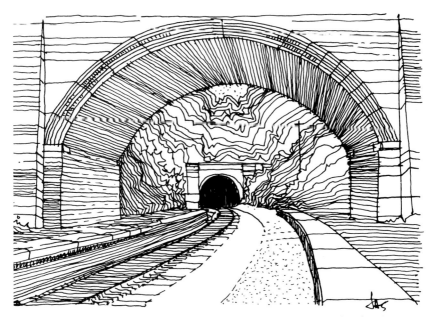

Sherwood Tunnel
North End

Drawn from a photograph taken in 1946

Nottingham Suburban Railway before the desolation, Friday 1st June 1951. The thrice-weekly goods train, pulled by G.N. 0.6.0 ST 68768, leaving Thorneywood for Daybrook. The photograph was taken from the public footbridge. (Photo: E.C. Haywood).

RCTS Rail-tour leaving Ashwells Tunnel on Great Northern Suburban line. Last passenger train on line. (Photo: T.G. Hepburn)   *(16/6/51)*

Thrice-weekly (MWFO) Nottingham Suburban Railway pick-up goods, ex Leen Valley Junction sidings on its outward journey to Thorneywood and back. This view was taken from Woodthorpe Drive bridge looking north towards Daybrook on 30th May 1951, just three months before the line closed. Note milepost 3 (from Trent Lane Junction) to left of the permanent way man, who is standing on the site of the old northbound track. Note also, in the distance, the distant signal (fixed) for Daybrook, the only remaining distant signal on the line. (Photo: E.C. Haywood). The locomotive is a Great Northern "J5" 0.6.0 5498.

CR 123 at Nottingham London Road Low Level Station on exhibition . Note "Royal Train Pilot". *(18/10/53)*

Northampton train leaving Nottingham London Road ex LNW 2-4-2T 6616. T.C. Hine's warehouse in background. *(7/6/39)*

An L.M.S. Market Harborough-Nottingham (London Road Low Level) local train crossing Radcliffe-on-Trent Viaduct, L.N.E.R. Midland 2-4-0 No. 162, 28 July 1932. (Photo: E.C. Haywood). The date when these signals were superseded by upper quadrants is not known, but the latter were certainly there in August 1936, erected on the Nottingham side of the bridge instead of as shown.

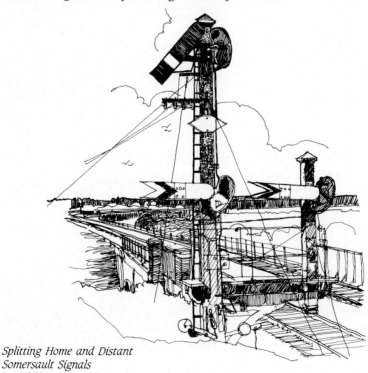

Splitting Home and Distant
Somersault Signals
Radcliffe-on-Trent from photograph taken in 1954.

NOTTINGHAM-DERBY
A Celebration of 150 years of Travel by Rail

OPENING

OF THE

BRANCH FROM NOTTINGHAM TO DERBY.

(From the Nottingham Review, Friday, May 31, 1839.)

We congratulate the inhabitants of this town and neighbourhood, on the progress which has been made towards: the completion of the Midland Counties' Railway. Convinced, as we have long been, that this new species of communication is destined to effect wonderful alterations and changes—in fact, a topographical revolution in our native country, we have viewed railroads as being of the utmost importance, and while we deeply regret that Nottingham has been left out of the great lines which traverse the kingdom, we will not now spend our time in unavailing regret, but rather rejoice in the additional medium of communication which is now about to be opened to the public.

The thousands who were attracted yesterday, to see the carriages take the first public journey, with the directors and their friends, specially invited upon the occasion, evince that there is a strong feeling of curiosity relative to this novel undertaking, for novel it is to great numbers in this town and neighbourhood, who never before witnessed the railway travelling, of which so much has appeared in the newspapers, and other publications, during the last few years. To gratify that curiosity as far as possible, we have collected a variety of information from different sources, and now proceed to give it to our readers.

THE RAILWAY STATION

Is situated in our beautiful and luxuriant Meadows. The front of the Station House is in a line with the west side of Carrington-street, from which it is separated by the Canal, over which, should the West-croft Inclosure Bill be carried, there will be a fine bridge, thus affording an easy access to the town. The Station House occupies about 450 square yards, being at the eastern extremity of the railway; and as it fronts the London-road, has from thence, Sneinton-hermitage, and Colwick-hill, a beautiful effect. It is built in the Grecian Doric style of architecture, with a stone facade, 90 feet in length, with Darley Dale stone from the quarry of Arthur Heathcoat, Esq. and is divided into a centre and two wings. The centre has an architrave and enriched consoler to the door and window, and a dentilated entablature on top, with

MIDLAND COUNTIES' RAILWAY.

Opening of the Branch Railway from Nottingham to Derby

THE STATION-HOUSE, IN NOTTINGHAM MEADOWS.

Here the passengers assemble, and take their places in the carriages, which are inside of the long building or shed, of which you see the outer wall, with eight circular-headed windows in a line.

THE ENGINE-HOUSE, AND CARRIAGES.

The chimney, sixty feet high, belongs to the stationary four-horse power high pressure steam-engine, described below. The engine-house serves as a depository for the loco-motive engines, here they are supplied with hot water from the tank at the end of the building, from which a pipe projects for that purpose, as seen in the engraving. First in the line of carriages is the "SUNBEAM" engine, attached to which is the tender, with coke for the fire. Next follows a second class carriage, or three carriages in one, with open windows; after this, two first class carriages, with glazed window, something like three coaches together, each coach containing six passengers, making eighteen in each carriage. In our picture we have next a second class carriage, and this is followed by a luggage truck, and a truck for live cattle.

stone balustrade, surmounted with a scroll and shield, bearing the arms of the Company. The two wings are plain pilaster, with a sunk panel and enriched guiloche in the parapet, which are carried up to conceal the roof of the wings, the roof the centre being concealed in like manner with the balustrade. The centre is devoted to the entrance-hall, and is 34 feet by 24½; and the south wing has a waiting room for ladies, 18 feet by 10; there is also a gentlemen's room, 23 feet by 17 feet, and second class waiting room, 16 feet by 17 feet; each room has a yard attached, with proper conveniences. The North wing is appropriated to the booking and parcel office, 12 feet by 31 feet, and the residence of the Chief Clerk, which contains parlour. 14 feet by 16 feet; kitchen, 16 feet by 9; and four bed rooms, with a pantry, scullery, coal-house, yard, and other offices. There is a double shed, 160 feet long by 35 feet wide, and 16 feet wide, with an iron roof supported on columns, and the North shed, next the Canal, is appropriated to the arrival line of rails, and a spare line for carriages. The South shed being appropriated, in like manner, for the departure line, and a spare line for carriages, a double line of rails being laid in each shed. There is a flagged platform in each shed, raised to the level of the bottom of the carriages, so as to enter or dismount with ease; that on the departure line of shed being 14 feet wide and 160 feet long; and that in the arrival shed being 6 feet wide, and descending (with four stone steps, the entire length of the shed) to the paved causeway, where the omnibus will be waiting the arrival of the trains. Adjoining the entrance gate, are the buildings appropriated to the Superintendent of Police, offices and waiting rooms for porters, &c. The quantity of land, about eighteen acres, is inclosed on the North and West sides with a substantial brick wall, and on the East side by the station-house, and on the South by the new channel of the Tinker's Leen, which has been diverted through the embankment by a bridge of two arches, 12 feet span. There are two entrances, one on the East side, by the Canal bridge, and the West entrance. By the station house, midway between, a bridge, 16 feet span, is building, so as a dock or branch can be made from the Canal, 50 feet wide and 250 feet long. On the North side of the line, about 250 yards from the station, stands the engine-house, which is 80 feet by 26 feet, with coke stove, 12 by 20 feet, with a tank 16 feet by 8—0 by 3 feet on top, supplied from a well sunk for the purpose. A smith's shop, lathe shop, and store-rooms, with engine-house for a four horse high pressure, occupy the back part of this station.

The engine is used for pumping, and turning a lathe; the chimney is about 60 feet high, and square to the top of the roof, and circular for the last forty feet. This building is brick, with stone sills and verge corners or gables; the windows are circular top, with guaged arches, and two pilasters coupled between each window, which entirely take away all appearance of flatness.

The road to Wilford is crossed on a level, where a neat lodge and gates are erected, for the security of passengers. Messrs. B. Drewry, T. Dale, Hall, and Wood, are the contractors for about £5675.

Chief Station Clerk—Mr. Lightfoot.
General Superintendent—Mr. Hutchinson.
Consulting Engineer—Charles Vignolles, Esq.
Engineer-in-chief—Thomas Woodhouse, Esq.
Secretary—J. F. Bell, Esq.

OPENING OF THE
NOTTINGHAM AND DERBY *RAILWAY,*

BY THE DIRECTORS & THEIR FRIENDS.

Yesterday, being the day appointed for the first public trip on the new railroad, the directors and their friends assembled at the station-house, in the Meadows, We arrived there about half-past eleven, and found that every preparation had been made, the four locomotive engines were in readiness, and were moving slowly backward and forward on the line, to the great delight and satisfaction of a multitude of beholders. There were twelve first class carriages, and eight second class, and for comfort and convenience, they surpass those upon the Manchester and Liverpool line.

The engines are beautiful specimens of mechanical ability, and in addition to the three already noticed, there was the MERSEY, made by Galloway and Co., of Manchester. The carriages were occupied by many of the principal inhabitants of the town. At twelve o'clock the fine band of the 5th Dragoons struck up an enlivening tune, and the scene at this moment was truly exhilirating. The day was uncommonly fine, the sun shone beautifully, thousands were assembled in the Meadows, to witness the sight, and on the other side, the wharfs, the tops of the houses, the Castle yard, and every place, where a view could be obtained, was crowded with spectators, anxious to witness a sight altogether novel to thousands in this town and neighborhood. Indeed, the town, in the morning seemed almost depopulated, and the streets were nearly deserted. It seemed a general holiday. The bells of the churches rang a merry peal, and all was hilarity and joy. Within the inclosure was thronged with the most respectable inhabitants of the town; the police-officers and the numerous servants of the establishment were attired in their new liveries, and every man at his post.

Precisely at half-past twelve, the first engine, with carriages attached, set off from the station. The second engine set off at twenty-seven minutes to one o'clock, the band playing "God save the Queen." With this we travelled, and therefore can note the time of its journey more accurately than the others. For the general outline of the interesting objects which every minute presented a fresh feature to the eye, we must refer to the ample details in our front page. We ought to notice, however, the thousands assembled on the hills in the Park, to gaze on this mighty triumph of mechanical skill; and indeed we may say, the road was lined in many places with admiring crowds, starting from amongst whom, ever and anon, appeared a dog, anxious to try his powers of speed by running by the side of this new racer, which in a few moments left the astonished animal in the distance. The cows generally remained quiescent; the horses seemed alarmed, and retreated to the farthest hedge; the calves and the sheep also ran away affrighted. The train reached the Beeston station-house in nine minutes; crossed the Erewash, and entered Derbyshire in thirteen minutes and a half: after passing Breaston, there was a stoppage of three minutes to take in a fresh supply of water, and reached Derby at

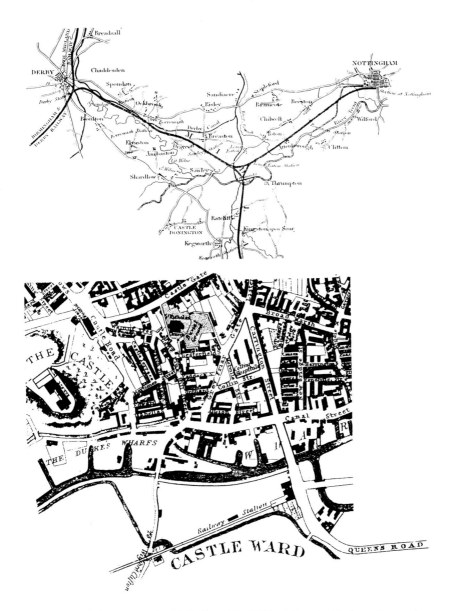

(Upper) Nottingham to Derby 1840 (from The Midland Counties Railway Companion 1840). (Lower) Nottingham's First Railway Station (from William Dearden's Map of Nottingham 1844).

"A temporary station is erected at Derby, on the West side of the Derwent, the same bridge being used by all the three Companies—North Midland, Birmingham and Derby, and Midland Counties. A new road is also made from the station at Derby, to the London-road, coming into it opposite the Infirmary."

nineteen minutes past one o'clock, thus performing the journey in forty-six minutes. We need scarcely add, that at Derby there was an excitement almost equal to that at Nottingham, thousands awaiting the arrival of the trains.

At Derby we stayed an hour and two minutes. The passengers left the carriages, and wandered about the town, and fain would we have paid a visit to the grand exhibition of the costly works of art and science, now to be seen at the Mechanics' Institute, Wardwick, but time would not allow. Next week, however, when the trains go three or four times a day, we doubt not many will avail themselves of the opportunity of inspecting the grandest exhibition of curiosities ever seen out of London. As it was, our time was limited; so stepping into the carriage again, we left Derby at twenty-nine minutes to three, and though at first, in consequence of the road not being quite perfect, the pace was slow, it soon increased, and we reached the station yard in Nottingham, at thirteen minutes past three, thus completing the journey back in forty-two minutes.

It seemed something like enchantment or a dream, to set our foot again so soon in Nottingham. Not an hour before, we had been walking in the streets of Derby, looking at All Saints and the well-known shot tower, admiring the new building erected for the Derbyshire Banking Company, and viewing the yet unfinished pile destined for a Post Office and Royal Hotel—and now, so soon and so easily, to find ourselves in Nottingham, seemed passing strange. But we had not much time for reflection. The directors had most handsomely provided a cold collation for the company; the ladies retired into their room, which was bountifully set out for the occasion, and the gentlemen made free at the long table, spread out under the shed for the carriages, provided most plenteously with substantial refreshments, which did great honor to the liberality of the directors. All appeared highly delighted with the treat, and such was the excellency of the arrangements, that the whole proceedings of the day passed off without any accident whatever, as far as our knowledge extends.

After the good things had been despatched, there were several speeches made by gentlemen from a distance; and at six o'clock, the company from Derby were invited to take their places in the carriages, and they were conveyed home in double quick time, the whole distance from Nottingham to Derby and back being performed in one hour and one minute, without including stoppages! This is indeed travelling by steam!

After the ladies and gentlemen had finished their repast, the workmen sat down at the same tables, and enjoyed an excellent dinner.

Each of the twelve first-class carriages, contain 18 passengers, and the eight second-class carriages contain 24 passengers. They were all full, and a number of persons sat upon other parts of the train, so that more than 500 individuals enjoyed the high treat of a trip to Derby and back again.

(From The Nottingham Review May-June 1839).

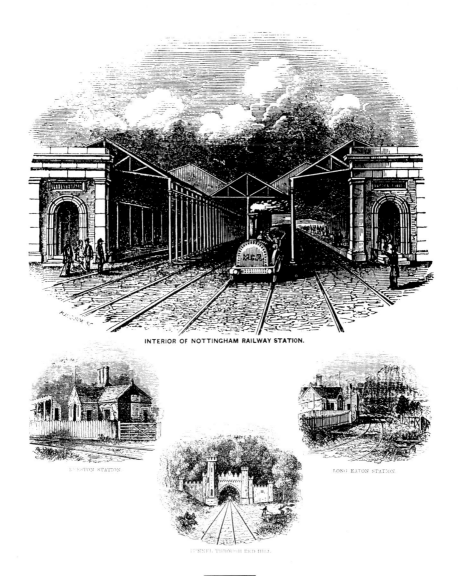

INTERIOR OF NOTTINGHAM RAILWAY STATION.

ILKESTON STATION.

LONG EATON STATION.

TUNNEL THROUGH RED HILL.

The Steam Engines are beautiful specimens of mechanical ingenuity, and skill, and will amply repay those who have a taste for, and are capable of appreciating, the talents of our first-rate mechanics.

The HAWK was made by Messrs. Stark and Fulton, of Glasgow; the largest wheel is 5 ft. 6 in. in diameter.

The SUNBEAM is from the establishment of Messrs. Jones, Turner, and Evans, of the Viaduct Foundry, Warrington; its wheel is of the same diameters as the HAWK.

Lastly, the ARIEL; this very neat engine was built by our neighbours, Messrs. Wright, Jessop, and Co., of the Butterly Works, the largest wheel is 5 ft. in diameter.

MIDLAND COUNTIES' RAILWAY.

NOTTINGHAM AND DERBY:

TIME TABLES,
&c. &c.

NOTTINGHAM TO DERBY. STATIONS.	1st, 2nd, & 3rd Class Carriages.	1st & 2nd Class Carriages.	1st & 2nd Class Carriages.	1st & 2nd Class Carriages.	1st, 2nd, & 3rd Class Carriages.	SUNDAY TRAINS. 1st, 2nd, & 3rd Class Carriages.	1st, 2nd, & 3rd Class Carriages.
	h. m.	h. m.	h. m.	h. m.	h. m.	h. m.	h. m.
NOTTINGHAM..........	7 0	10 30	1 30	3 0	7 30	7 0	7 30
BEESTON	7 6	10 36		3 6	7 36	7 6	7 36
LONG EATON	7 15	10 45	1 40	3 15	7 45	7 15	7 45
SAWLEY..............	7 25	10 55		3 25	7 55	7 25	7 55
BOROWASH	7 35	11 5		3 35	8 5	7 35	8 5
SPONDON	7 40	11 10		3 40	8 10	7 40	8 10
DERBY................	7 45	11 15	2 0	3 45	8 15	7 45	8 15

DERBY TO NOTTINGHAM.							
DERBY....................	6 10	9 15	1 10	4 0	8 30	6 10	6 30
SPONDON..............		9 21	1 16	4 6	8 36	6 16	6 36
BOROWASH		9 25	1 20	4 10	8 40	6 20	6 40
SAWLEY		9 35	1 30	4 20	8 50	6 30	6 50
LONG EATON		9 45	1 40	4 30	9 0	6 40	7 0
BEESTON		9 55	1 50	4 40	9 10	6 50	7 10
NOTTINGHAM	6 35	9 60	1 55	4 45	9 15	6 55	7 15

CHARGES FOR CARRIAGES, &c

Private Carriages between Nottingham and Derby, 10s.—Two wheel Carriages, 6s. One Horse between Nottingham and Derby, 7s.—Two, 10s.—Horse Box, 13s. Waggon for conveyance of Cattle, Pigs, &c., 10s.—Dogs, 1s. Passengers in or on Private Carriages pay 2nd Class Fares.—Children under 10, half-price.

FOR CATTLE, &c.

Oxen, if carried in a Horse Box, same price as Horses; if in a Waggon, each 5s. A Calf, Sheep, or Pig, each, 1s. 6d.; if more than one, 1s. per head.
A person may hire a Waggon of the Company on payment of 10s., and put as many of the above as belong to him, and accompany them himself, on paying Third Class Fare.

* London and Liverpool Trains.

MIDLAND COUNTIES' RAILWAY.—NOTTINGHAM AND DERBY.

TABLE OF FARES.

STATIONS.	NOTTINGHAM. CLASS 1	2	3	BEESTON. CLASS 1	2	3	LONG EATON. CLASS 1	2	3	SAWLEY. CLASS 1	2	3	BOROWASH. CLASS 1	2	3	SPONDON. CLASS 1	2	3
	s. d.	s. d.	s. d.	s. d.	s. d.	s. d.	s. d.	s. d.	s. d.	s. d.	s. d.	s. d.	s. d.	s. d.	s. d.	s. d.	s. d.	s. d.
Beeston	1 0	0 6																
Long Eaton	1 6	1 0		1 0	0 6													
Sawley	2 0	1 3		1 6	1 0		1 0	0 6										
Borowash........	2 6	1 6		2 0	1 3		1 6	1 0		1 0	0 6							
Spondon	3 0	1 9		2 6	1 3		2 0	1 0		1 0	0 9		1 0	0 6				
Derby..........	3 6	2 0	1 0	3 0	1 6		2 0	1 3		2 0	1 0		1 0	0 6		1 0	0 6	

3rd Class Passengers are Booked only at Derby and Nottingham.

RATES OF PARCELS TO AND FROM NOTTINGHAM AND DERBY.

Not exceeding 14lbs. 6d.; above 14lbs. and under 28lbs. 9d.; above 28lbs. and under 56lbs. 1s.

VAN GOODS, (TO ONE ADDRESS)—Above 56lbs. and under 112lbs., 1s. 6d.; Above 112lbs., 1s. 6d. per cwt.

The Rates for Parcels and Goods include delivery and all other charges except the customary 2d. for booking; a label stating the sum to be paid for carriage will be affixed to each Parcel, and any servant of the Company taking more than is thereon expressed will be dismissed.

NOTICE.—The Company will not be responsible for Parcels or Goods above the value of £10, unless declared as such at the time of booking, and entered, and insurance paid for accordingly.

A Van Leaves Nottingham for Derby, London, Birmingham, Liverpool, and Manchester, at Half-past Seven every Evening.—Carriage to London—Small Parcels under 18 lb., 1s. 6d.; above, 1d. per lb.

☞ Persons desirous of their Parcels going by Railway, are requested to mark them conspicuously, " Per Railway."

(From The Nottingham and Derby Railway Companion 1839).